Who Pooped in the Park?

Written by Gary D. Robson
Illustrated by Robert Rath

FARCOUNTRY
PRESS

To my incredible wife, Kathy.
- Gary

For Lucy and Thomas, my poop experts.
- Robert

ISBN: 978-1-56037-339-1

© 2006 Farcountry Press
Text © 2006 Gary D. Robson
Illustrations © 2006 Farcountry Press

Who Pooped? is a registered trademark of Farcountry Press.

For more information about our books, write Farcountry Press, P.O. Box 5630, Helena, MT 59604; call (800) 821-3874; or visit www.farcountrypress.com.

Manufactured by
Versa Press, Inc.
Spring Bay Road/Route 26
East Peoria, IL 61611-9788
in July 2018

Book design by Robert Rath.

 Produced and printed in the United States of America.

22 21 20 19 18   3 4 5 6 7

Library of Congress Cataloging-in-Publication Data

Robson, Gary D.
   Who pooped in the park?. Shenandoah National Park / [Gary D. Robson, Robert Rath].
      p. cm.
   ISBN-13: 978-1-56037-339-1
   1. Animal tracks—Virginia—Shenandoah National Park—Juvenile literature. I. Rath, Robert. II. Title.
QL768.R644 2006
591.9755'9—dc22

                                    2005016665

"Dad? I have to go to the bathroom."
Michael squirmed in the back seat.

"We'll be at our campground
any minute," said Dad.
"We're in Shenandoah
National Park now."

3

"He's just nervous," said Michael's sister. "He thinks a bear's gonna eat him." She growled at Michael and made her fingers look like claws.

"Stop it, Emily," said Mom. "Nobody is getting eaten by anything."

Michael was very excited about the trip,
but Emily was right. He *was* nervous.

He had just read a book about grizzly bears.
He knew how big they could get.

And he was afraid that a hungry bear would eat
just about anything—maybe even a boy.

"I *am* kind of scared of grizzly bears," admitted Michael.

"Don't worry," Dad told him. "There are no grizzlies around here. Just black bears."

Mom reached back and held Michael's hand. She said, "We'll show you how to count a black bear's toes and never get close enough to be scared."

"Here's our campsite. Let's set up the tent. Then we can go for a walk and we'll show you what we mean," Dad said.

Michael was pretty worried about bear toes, but tried not to show it.

"Let's hurry!" said Emily. "I want to see some animals!"

Once the tent was up, the whole family went for a hike.

Emily started to complain before they even left the campground. "I haven't seen any animals yet. Maybe there aren't any here!"

"Sure there are," said Dad. "Let's see what we can learn about them from their *sign*."

"Sign?" said Michael. "You mean like a sign at the zoo?"

WHITE-TAILED DEER

TURKEY

BOBCAT

Dad smiled. "In this case, a sign is a clue that an animal has left behind. Look there by the stream bank."

"All of these signs tell a story," said Mom. "There was an animal digging here, catching and eating crayfish. Its tracks show that it has five toes."

"A raccoon was here," Mom said.

"We have those around home, don't we?" asked Michael.

"Raccoons live almost everywhere in the United States," answered Dad. "They can swim and climb trees, and they eat all kinds of food, including fruit, nuts, insects, eggs, and small animals such as these crayfish."

the STRAIGHT
POOP

Raccoons are very clever and skilled. They can work doorknobs and take the lids off of garbage cans.

"And here's some raccoon poop, right?" said Michael.

"Yes, but be careful not to touch it," Mom answered. "You can get sick from touching animal poop—especially raccoon poop."

"See, Michael," said Dad. "We don't have to get up close to an animal to learn about it. Instead of a close encounter of the *scary* kind, we'll have a close encounter of the *poopy* kind."

Everybody laughed, and Mom made a gross-out face.

"These raccoon tracks over here
are a lot smaller," said Emily.

"That's because they aren't from a raccoon,"
said Dad. "Notice that the front foot only has four
toes? I think you're looking at squirrel tracks."

"And the squirrel is looking at you,"
laughed Mom, as a gray squirrel
ran up a tree and scolded
them loudly.

"See the squirrel scat next to the tracks?" Dad asked.

"*Scat?*" asked Emily. "What's *scat?*"

"It's the word hikers and trackers use for animal poop," said Mom.

"Dad! Mom! Look over here! I found bunny scat!" yelled Michael. "It's just like what we find in Fluffy's cage."

"We came all the way to Shenandoah National Park for that?" grumbled Emily. "Michael's bunny makes plenty of poop at home."

the STRAIGHT POOP

Rabbits eat their own scat! They do this to get as much nutrition from the food as they can. The little brown balls are scat that's already been through twice.

Dad said, "Around here, it's probably a cottontail rabbit."

"And these are its tracks?" Emily asked.
She was starting to get a bit less grumpy.

"Right," said Mom. "There are four toes on the front *and* back feet, but it's hard to tell sometimes because their feet are so fuzzy that you can't see their toes in the tracks very well."

RABBIT
TRACKS

FRONT
FEET

BACK
FEET

"There it goes!" said Dad, as Mom and Emily looked on.

While everybody else looked at the rabbit, Michael was more interested in the scat.

"I found some even bigger bunny poop here," he announced.

DEER SCAT:
SPRING / SUMMER

DEER SCAT:
FALL / WINTER

RABBIT SCAT

JELLYBEANS

"This scat is from a deer, not a rabbit," said Mom.

"You can tell by the shape." added Dad. "Rabbit poop is almost round, but deer scat is shaped more like jellybeans."

the STRAIGHT POOP

Deer scat looks different in the spring because deer eat more fresh green plants then.

Michael found some marks in the dirt. "Are these deer tracks?" he asked.

"Yes!" said Mom. "They're from a white-tailed deer. See how they're split? Deer hooves have two parts."

"What are these little marks?" asked Emily. She was starting to get interested.

DEW CLAW

"Those are from its dew claws," said Mom. "They're little claws behind the hoof. Dew claws sometimes show in deer tracks in soft ground. Lots of other animals have dew claws, too, including cats and dogs."

"Oh, no!" said Michael. Here's one
of its antlers! Did a bear eat the deer?"
Michael looked around nervously.

Dad bent down by the antler.
"Oh, no, the deer didn't get eaten.
This is called a 'shed' antler.
Their antlers fall off every
winter, and the deer grow
a new, bigger set
the next year."

the STRAIGHT POOP

Female deer, elk, and moose
don't grow antlers. Reindeer
are the only members of the deer
family in which both males and
females have antlers.

"This deer was in a hurry, though," said Mom, as she studied the ground.

Michael and Emily went over to look.

"How can you tell?" said Emily. She was having fun finding all the clues the animals left behind.

"The hoofprints get very far apart here," Mom explained, "and the back prints are in front of the front prints."

"It was walking backwards?" said Emily.

"No, it was galloping. Something scared the deer and it was moving fast." Mom said.

BACK
HOOVES

FRONT
HOOVES

WALKING GALLOPING

GALLOPING

24

"Here's what scared the deer," Dad said. "There are bobcat tracks all around here."

"Bobcats eat deer?" asked Michael.

Dad answered, "Most of the time bobcats eat rabbits and mice, but they're great hunters. Bobcats sometimes catch deer, even though the deer are much bigger than they are."

"Will the bobcat hurt us?" asked Michael. He looked around nervously.

"You don't need to be scared," Mom answered. "Bobcats are pretty shy, and they don't come out much in the daytime."

the STRAIGHT POOP

Since cats can retract their claws, bobcat tracks don't show claw marks.

"That's right," added Dad. "They're very good hunters, but they don't hunt people."

BOBCAT TRACKS

BOBCAT SCAT

the STRAIGHT POOP

Bobcats bury their scat just like house cats. You'll rarely see bobcat scat in the wild.

"Here's some really big scat," said Michael.

"I know what that is," Emily said excitedly. "That's horse poop!"

"Yes," said Mom. "And here are some hoofprints from the horse, too."

"Those are funny-looking hoofprints," said Michael.

the STRAIGHT POOP

Horses can walk while they poop, but they stop and stand still to pee.

"Horses don't have split hooves like deer and elk, Michael" said Dad. "There's just one part."

"I think he's talking about the horseshoes," said Mom. "They make the hoofprints look different."

"Let's head up the trail toward those rocks," she added. "I think we might see something new up there."

the STRAIGHT POOP

Horses that are ridden a lot have metal shoes attached to their hooves to protect them from wear. The shape of the shoe shows in the horse tracks.

ELK DEER HORSE HORSE WITH HORSESHOE

Sure enough, the kids spotted something interesting when they reached the rocks.

"What are these white streaks on the rocks over here?" he asked.

"That's called guano," said Dad.

the STRAIGHT
POOP

Guano makes very good fertilizer. People buy bags of it to spread in their gardens to keep their plants healthy.

the STRAIGHT POOP

Bats sleep hanging upside-down and like to perch in caves, trees, and holes in the rock.

"I know what that is!" exclaimed Emily. "We learned about it in school. Guano is bat poop!"

"Right," said Mom. "There are a lot of different bats in Shenandoah National Park. The most common is the big brown bat."

"Do they suck blood like vampires?" said Michael with a shudder.

"Oh no, they're just tiny bats that eat bugs," said Mom with a smile. "There are no vampire bats around here."

the STRAIGHT POOP

Even though they're called big brown bats, they are smaller than robins.

Emily noticed something strange on the tree.

"Is this more bat poop?" she asked.

"That poop is from an owl," Dad said. He looked down at the ground below the tree and added, "See these tracks with two toes pointing forward and two pointing back, and the owl pellets around the base of the tree?"

"Owl pellets?" said Emily.

"Owls eat their prey whole," explained Dad. "The parts they can't digest, like hair and bones, get coughed up in a pellet like this."

the STRAIGHT POOP

Studying owl pellets is a great way to find out what owls eat. Barred owls dine on a wide variety of small animals, including mice, squirrels, rats, snakes, birds, frogs, fish, crayfish, grasshoppers, small rabbits, and even bats.

The kids took one look and said, "Yuck!"

"What kind
of owl are these pellets
from?" Michael asked.

"It's hard to tell without seeing it,"
said Dad, "but the tracks and pellets
are about the right size for a barred owl."

the STRAIGHT POOP

Owls see very well at night, but they aren't blind during the day, as some people believe. They see just fine then, too.

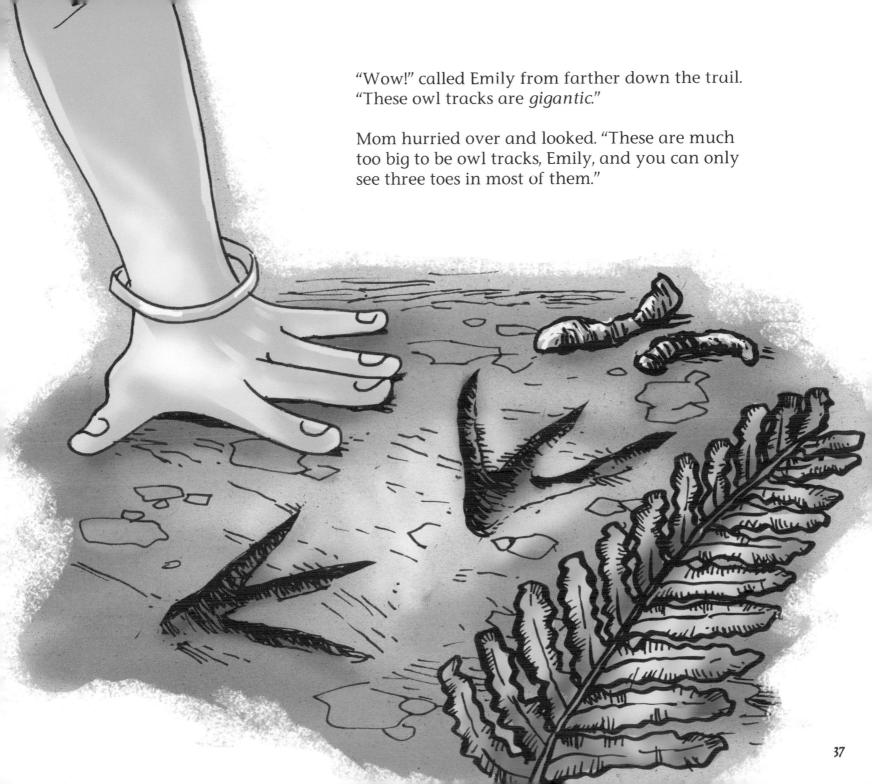

"Wow!" called Emily from farther down the trail. "These owl tracks are *gigantic*."

Mom hurried over and looked. "These are much too big to be owl tracks, Emily, and you can only see three toes in most of them."

"These are wild turkey tracks," Dad said.

the STRAIGHT POOP

Benjamin Franklin wanted to make the wild turkey the American national bird instead of the bald eagle.

"Whoa! What happened to this tree?" asked Michael.

"Something was sharpening its claws, and if you look how high those scratch marks go, it was pretty big!" said Mom.

"It's not just the animal that's big," said Emily. "Look at the size of this poop!"

"It looks like we found your black bear," said Mom. "Let's see what you learned today. What can you figure out about this bear?"

"It's been eating plants," said Emily, "because there's no hair or bones in this poop."

"Good job!" Mom said. "What else?"

the STRAIGHT POOP

Black bears eat almost anything. They mostly live on leaves, nuts, berries, insects, twigs, and honey, but they also hunt small animals and fish.

"Dad, it must be as tall as you, and it has really long claws," said Michael.

"Here's its footprint," said Michael. "The track is really big, and it has five toes like a raccoon instead of four like a bobcat."

"We told you you'd be able to count a black bear's toes," laughed Dad.

"It rubbed off some black hair on the tree," said Emily. "That must be why they call them black bears!"

"All of the black bears in Shenandoah National Park are black," explained Mom. "But in western areas, black bears can be all different colors. They can be black, brown, or cinnamon-colored. Some black bears are almost white."

As the family ate dinner that night, everyone talked about how much fun they had.

"We didn't see very many animals," said Emily, "but it seemed like we did!"

Everyone laughed when Michael said, "And I didn't get scared once!"

TRACKS and

BLACK BEAR	BOBCAT	RACCOON	COTTONTAIL RABBIT	GRAY SQUIRREL

Tracks are large with five visible toes and claws.	Tracks show four toes; claw marks are usually not visible.	Tracks are large for the animal's size. Five bulbous toes.	Four toes on front track and five on back.	Four toes on front track and five on back.

Scat changes depending on diet but usually contains vegetation.	Scat tends to break apart and is often buried.	Scat is blunt on ends and may contain dangerous parasites. DON'T TOUCH RACCOON SCAT!	Scat is small and round.	Scat is tiny, long ovals, much smaller than cottontail rabbit's.

SCAT NOTES

HORSE

Tracks are much larger than deer tracks, and hooves aren't split.

Scat is in chunks, with roughage from vegetation often visible.

BIG BROWN BAT

Bats rarely land on soft ground to leave tracks.

Scat is runny and white.

BARRED OWL

Tracks show four toes: two pointing forward and two pointing backward or sideways.

Scat is runny and white. "Cough pellets" contain fur and bones.

WHITE-TAILED DEER

Tracks show a pointed split hoof.

Scat is oval-shaped like jellybeans.

WILD TURKEY

Tracks are larger than owl tracks, with back-pointing toe often not showing.

Scat is long and narrow. Fresh scat is brown in the middle and greenish white on the ends.

ABOUT the AUTHOR and ILLUSTRATOR

GARY D. ROBSON

Gary Robson lives in Montana, not far from Yellowstone National Park. He has written dozens of books and hundreds of articles, mostly related to science, nature, and technology.
www.robson.org/gary

ROBERT RATH

is a book designer and illustrator living in Bozeman, Montana. Although he has worked with Scholastic Books, Lucasfilm, and The History Channel, his favorite project is keeping up with his family.

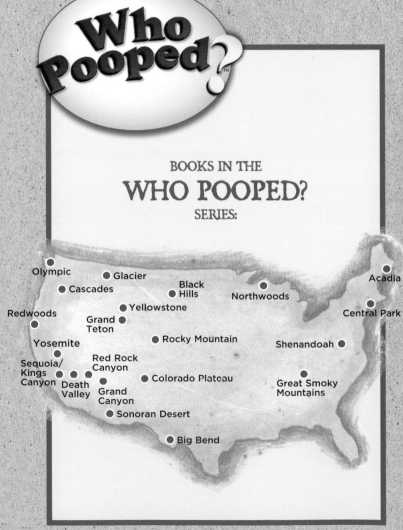

Who Pooped?

BOOKS IN THE
WHO POOPED?
SERIES:

Olympic
Cascades
Glacier
Black Hills
Northwoods
Acadia
Redwoods
Yellowstone
Grand Teton
Central Park
Yosemite
Rocky Mountain
Shenandoah
Sequoia/Kings Canyon
Red Rock Canyon
Death Valley
Grand Canyon
Colorado Plateau
Great Smoky Mountains
Sonoran Desert
Big Bend